The Rourke Guide
to State Symbols

STATE CAPITALS

Tracy Maurer

The Rourke Press, Inc.
Vero Beach, Florida 32964

PHOTO CREDITS:
page 6 © Bob Rink; page 9 © Denver Metro Visitor' Bureau; page 11 © Delaware Tourism Office; page 17 © Banayote Photo; page 19 © Louisiana Office of Tourism; page 20 © Maine Office of Tourism; page 23 © Travel Bureau, MDC; page 24 © Minnesota Historical Society; page 26 © Donnie Sexton; page 27 © P. Michael Whye; page 28 © Nevada Tourism; **page 30 © Mark Nohl**; page 32 © Jim Davis & the Raleigh Convention & Visitor's Bureau; page 34© Oklahoma City Convention and Visitor's Bureau; page 36 © Jeff Hixon, Commonwealth Media Services; page 39 © SD Tourism/C.C.; page 41 © Michael A. Murphy; page 43 © Vermont Travel Division; page 48 © Wyoming Division of Tourism; page 7 © Little Rock Chamber of Commerce; page 13 © Georgia Division of Tourism; page 14 © Hawaii Visitor's Bureau;page 48 © Wyoming Division of Tourism; page 16 © Springfield's Visitor's Bureau; page 17 © Iowa Division of Tourism; page 19 © Creative Services Photography; page 21 © Tom Darden—MD State Archives; page 24 © MI Division of Tourism; page 25 © MO Division of Tourism; page 28 © Kenneth Leidner; page 31 © NYS Dept. of Economic Development; page 32 © ND Film Commission; page 33 © Capital Square Revue Board; page 45 © WA Division of Archives; page 46 © Craig Lopetz;
From Unicorn Stock photo:
page 5 © Dennis Macdonald; page 6 © Alice M. Prescott; page 8 © Gerald Lim; pages 10, 12, 37, 38 © Andre Jenny; page 18 © Arni Katz; pages 22, 29, 47 © Joe Sohm; page 35 © Karen Holsinger Mullen; pages 40, 44 © Jeff Greenberg; page 15 © James Fly; page 42 © Jim Hays

COVER ILLUSTRATION: Jim Spence

CREATIVE SERVICES:
East Coast Studios, Merritt Island, Florida

EDITORIAL SERVICES:
Janice L. Smith for Penworthy

REF
973
Mau

Library of Congress Cataloging-in-Publication Data

Maurer, Tracy, 1965-
   State Capitals / Tracy Maurer.
      p. cm. — (The Rourke guide to state symbols)
   Includes index.
   Summary: Briefly describes the capital city of each state, its history, and its capitol building.
   ISBN 1-57103-296-7
   1. United States—History, Local Juvenile literature. 2. Capitals (Cities)—United States Juvenile literature. 3. Cities and towns—United States Juvenile literature. 4. State governments—United States Juvenile literature. 5. Capitols Juvenile literature. [1. Capitals (Cities) 2. Cities and towns. 3. Capitols.] I. Title. II. Series.
E180.M38 1999
973—dc21   99-31455
                                                                              CIP

Printed in the USA

Table of Contents

INTRODUCTION

When each of the fifty states joined the United States of America, the new state named one of its cities as the capital. Capital, meaning the city where the government meets, is spelled differently than the capitol, or building where the government meets. All fifty capitals and fifty capitols tell much about their states.

In the 1800s when most states joined the Union, people traveled by foot or horses. The capitals needed to be easy to reach. Often, the city with the most people and businesses became the capital.

Because the states were new, sometimes no cities existed yet. In such cases, people simply guessed which cities would become important. If another city grew larger or more important than the old capital, some states named new capitals. Many states have changed capitals over the years.

Capitals also changed because of fires. When a capitol burned, it was usually rebuilt in the same place. But sometimes the capital moved to a new city.

Today, cars, trains and airplanes let people travel quickly anywhere. Location is less important. Over time, certain cities have grown larger and more famous than their state's capital. This explains why sometimes the capital is not the most well-known city in the state. Famous or not, all of the capitals are still very important.

ALABAMA
Capital: Montgomery

History:

Alabama changed its capital four times before finally settling on Montgomery in 1847. The original capitol burned only two years after the building opened. A new capitol with grand, white columns replaced it. Called the "Cradle of the Confederacy," Montgomery briefly served as the capital of the Confederate States of America when the Civil War began in 1861. Today this busy city on the Alabama River is also the Montgomery County seat, or place from which local governmental authority is exercised.

ALASKA

Capital: Juneau

History:

A gold rush in 1880 created the city of Harrisburg. A year later prospector Joe Juneau bought votes from local miners to change the city's name to Juneau. Juneau became the capital of the Alaskan territory in 1900 and it remained the capital when Alaska became a state in 1959. Juneau merged with the island town of Douglas in 1970, making its 3,108 square miles the United State's largest city in area.

ARIZONA

Capital: Phoenix

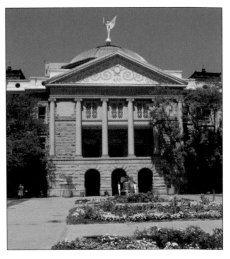

History:

White settlers named Phoenix, a desert city, for the legendary sun-bird that rose from its own ashes. Early farmers raised fruit, cotton and cattle with only an average of seven inches of rain each year. In the 1880s, the Arizona territory moved its capital from Prescott to Tucson and then back to Prescott. Phoenix was finally decided on in 1889 and a stunning capitol was built from local materials. Today, Phoenix is the state's largest city.

6

ARKANSAS

Capital: Little Rock

History:

Little Rock began as a trading post in 1722. Its location on the Arkansas River made it an ideal meeting spot. In 1821, Little Rock became the territory's capital. It kept the title when Arkansas joined the Union. The present capitol opened in 1916. Today Little Rock is the state's largest city. It serves as a meeting place for government, business, artists and students.

CALIFORNIA
Capital: Sacramento

History:
Sacramento originally was a trading post on the banks of the Sacramento and American Rivers. Riverboat traffic and the California gold rush helped the city thrive. Sacramento also grew because the Pony Express and California's first railroad ended there. Sacramento was named California's capital in 1854. The granite state capitol building looks a bit like the nation's Capitol in Washington, D.C. Built in 1874, it was later reworked to withstand earthquakes. Many people visit the beautiful capitol every year and enjoy the Capitol Museum tours.

COLORADO

Capital: Denver

History:

In the 1800s, fortune hunters flocked to two mining camps on the Rocky Mountain prairie. The camps quickly grew into the city of Denver, which became the state capital in 1876. It took many years to build the fine capitol. Copper on its dome turned green and in 1908 it was covered with 200 ounces of gold. The world's only known red marble, mined southwest of Pueblo and no longer available, gives the capitol its rare color.

CONNECTICUT

Capital: Hartford

History:

In the 1630s, English Puritans took over a Dutch settlement near what is today Hartford. They formed the Connecticut Colony and adopted what may have been the world's first written constitution. From 1701 to 1875, Hartford and New Haven shared the title of capital for the colony and later the state. A marble and granite capitol now stands in Hartford. Called the "Insurance City," Hartford has more insurance company headquarters than any other city. Hartford has become a major center for business, the arts and education.

DELAWARE

Capital: Dover

History:

Delaware is called "The First State" because it was the first of the original 13 states to ratify, or approve, the Constitution. But Delaware was a state even before that. In 1776, Delaware named New Castle its capital. The capital moved to Dover a year later. Today, Dover is also the seat of Kent County—one of just three counties in the second-smallest state.

FLORIDA

Capital: Tallahassee

History:

Tallahassee became Florida's capital in 1823 even before it was a town. The site was chosen because it stood midway between St. Augustine and Pensacola. Three log cabins served as the first capitol. The town quickly grew around them. A limestone building begun in 1826 was replaced in 1845 by the brick building now known as the "Old Capitol." Today's Capitol Complex, a 22-story office building, opened in 1977. It houses all the branches of government. The Old Capitol was saved from the wrecking ball and now welcomes visitors to its Museum of Florida History.

GEORGIA

Capital: Atlanta

History:

A railroad's southern end created the city of Terminus. Later called Marthasville and finally named Atlanta in 1847, the city's buildings burned in 1864 during the Civil War. Atlanta recovered and became the state capital in 1868. A graceful capitol decked in Georgia marble opened in 1889. A 2,000-pound Miss Freedom statue tops the capitol's gilded dome. Today, Atlanta is a major transportation center and has become a leading Southern city.

HAWAII

Capital: Honolulu

History:

Polynesians settled Hawaii between 300 and 600 A.D. Kings and queens ruled the chain of eight main islands for centuries. Honolulu, on the island of Oahu, was named the kingdom's capital in 1845. The kingdom ended in 1898. When Hawaii became a U.S. territory in 1900, Honolulu remained its capital. Today, Honolulu is still the state's major city and port. It welcomes millions of tourists each year.

IDAHO

Capital: Boise

History:

Boise began near the Boise River where the Oregon Trail and a mining route met. In 1865, Boise became the territorial capital. A red brick capitol was finished in 1886. This building was replaced by Idaho's current capitol, which opened in 1912. Idaho's own sandstone, shaped like logs, covers the outside walls of the capitol's first level. A bronzed solid-copper eagle perches on the capitol's dome. Hot geothermal water from a deep natural artesian well heats the capitol and all the buildings on the Capitol Mall.

ILLINOIS

Capital: Springfield

History:

The Illinois government has worked in six capitols since the state named Kaskaskia its first capital. The capital moved to Vandalia in 1820. Vandalia hosted four capitols before Illinois voters chose the more central city of Springfield as the capital in 1839. The government quickly outgrew its fifth capitol, and work on the present capitol began in 1868.

Abraham Lincoln lived in Springfield from 1837 to 1861. Every year thousands of people visit Springfield's many historic sites, which include Lincoln's home and his tomb.

INDIANA

Capital: Indianapolis

History:

Settlers founded Indianapolis in 1820 along the White River. Five years later, Indianapolis replaced Corydon as the state's capital. City planners laid out the streets like a wheel with Monument Circle at the center and the capitol nearby. Indianapolis grew quickly when the National Road and the railroad arrived by 1847. Today, five interstate highways meet in Indianapolis and the city is called the "Crossroads of America."

IOWA

Capital: Des Moines

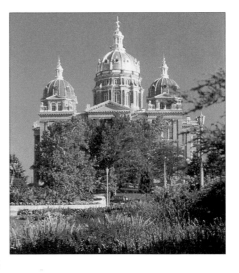

History:

Iowa's first capital was Iowa City. Des Moines, with its more central location, became the new capital in 1857. Workers laid the capitol's cornerstone in 1871. A harsh winter crumbled many of the foundation's stones and a second cornerstone was laid in 1873. This building opened in January 1884. Today's updated capitol features a 23-karat gilded dome 398 steps up from the ground, a marble interior and 27 fireplaces.

KANSAS

Capital: Topeka

History:
Anti-slavery colonists led by Charles Robinson and Cyrus Holliday settled Topeka in 1854. Trouble followed them there. Free-soil and pro-slavery groups fought in the city even before the Civil War. Topeka became the state's capital in 1861. After the Civil War, work began on the capitol and continued for 37 years. Today, the peaceful city of Topeka is one of the largest cities in Kansas.

KENTUCKY

Capital: Frankfort

History:

Six years before Kentucky won statehood, Frankfort became the capital. This historic city has built four capitols since then. In 1904, the third building became too small. At this time, Lexington and Louisville each tried to replace Frankfort as the

capital. But Frankfort kept the title and work began on its newest capitol. Huge marble stairways, detailed sculptures and grand windows still inspire as much awe today as they did when the building opened in January 1910.

LOUISIANA

Capital: Baton Rouge

History:

The 1803 Louisiana Purchase gave Baton Rouge to the United States. The city has served as the state's capital except during the Civil War. Today the nation's tallest state capitol looks out over Baton Rouge. It stands 450 feet high. A grand staircase with one step

for each of the first 48 states leads to the entrance. Alaska and Hawaii were added to the top step when they became states.

MAINE

Capital: Augusta

History:

The first white settlers to call Maine their home arrived in the 1620s. Maine did not win its statehood for another two hundred years. Massachusetts governed Maine until 1820. Portland was the first capital until 1831, when Augusta became the capital. Augusta's location in south central Maine on the Kennebec River puts the capital midway between the larger cities of Portland and Bangor.

MARYLAND

Capital: Annapolis

History:

Annapolis became Maryland's capital in 1794 when the colony moved it from St. Mary's City. The historic Maryland State House in Annapolis is the oldest state capitol still used for state government. Workers began building it in 1772. Slowed by the American Revolution, they did not finish until 1779. The Continental Congress met there from November 1783 to August 1874, making the Maryland State House the only state capitol to also serve as the nation's capitol.

MASSACHUSETTS

Capital: Boston

History:

The first Massachusetts State House was built in 1712. It still stands in Boston, the state's largest city. Work began on the second capitol building in 1795. It sits on Beacon Hill, land that John Hancock once used for a pasture. The capitol's shingled dome began leaking not long after it was built. Paul Revere's company covered the dome in copper to stop the leaks. In 1872, the dome was gilded. A pinecone, not a pineapple as some people think, tops the dome. This 18th-century brick building still exists as the main part of today's State House.

MICHIGAN

Capital: Lansing

History:

Settlers started the city of Michigan in the state's Lower Peninsula in 1837. They renamed it Lansing when the city became the capital in 1871. The historic capitol in the city center looks much like the U.S. Capitol. It opened in 1879 and the state's government has met there since then. In 1899, Ransom E. Olds began making automobiles in Lansing. Today the city is still a leading automobile builder.

MINNESOTA

Capital: St. Paul

History:

St. Paul's first capitol was built in 1853, but it burned in 1881. Two years later, a second capitol was built at the same location. The government quickly outgrew it. Work began on today's capitol in 1896 and the building opened in 1904. Its 220-foot-high dome is the world's largest unsupported marble dome. The Mississippi River separates the "Twin Cities," St. Paul and Minneapolis.

MISSISSIPPI

Capital: Jackson

History:

From 1822 to 1839, the state government met in a small brick capitol in Jackson. Work began on the second capitol in 1833. It wasn't finished until 1840. A new capitol opened in 1903. A gilded copper eagle with a 15-foot wingspan tops the capitol dome. Traditionally, all the lights in the building glow on the first day of each legislative session—that's 4,700 bright bulbs!

MISSOURI

Capital: Jefferson City

History:

In 1821, the little town of Jefferson City on the Missouri River became the state's capital. Its central location made it easy for legislators to meet there. Daniel M. Boone, the famous frontiersman's son, laid out Jefferson City in 1822. It took seven years to build the current capitol, which opened in 1918. Murals by the famous American painters Newell Convers Wyeth and Thomas Hart Benton hang in the capitol.

MONTANA

Capital: Helena

History:

When Montana became a state, Helena was named the capital. The city of Anaconda argued that it should hold the honor. A vote in 1894 settled the nasty dispute. The capitol opened in 1902. No one knows if the "Goddess of Liberty" on the copper dome was really made for the capitol. The company that sent the statue lost its records in a fire. The capitol's builders wanted a statue, so they claimed it.

NEBRASKA

Capital: Lincoln

History:

The city of Lincoln, or Lancaster as it was first named, began in 1864. Three years later, the capital moved to Lincoln from Omaha. The fifth and present capitol looks unlike any other in the world. A gilded dome caps its 400-foot tower. People can see the tower from miles away. William Jennings Bryan, the history-making politician, lived in Lincoln from 1887 to 1921. Visitors may tour his home there.

NEVADA

Capital: Carson City

History:

The Capitol Complex Plaza in the heart of Carson City once stood as a dusty field. The city founders set aside ten acres for the capitol when they laid out the town in 1858. But eleven years passed before work began. Today, several other important state buildings have joined the handsome sandstone capitol in the Plaza. These include the Legislative Building, Supreme Court, and State Library and Archives.

NEW HAMPSHIRE

Capital: Concord

History:

New Hampshire joined the Union in 1788, but the present capitol wasn't built in Concord until 1816. Workers used granite from Concord's own quarries. A large, gilded wooden eagle topped the capitol's dome. A weatherproof metal eagle later replaced it. Over the years, the city of Manchester made two major bids to become the capital. The legislature rejected the state's largest city in favor of Concord.

NEW JERSEY

Capital: Trenton

History:

In 1679, a settlement called The Falls began along the Delaware River. Later called Stacy's Mills and then Trenton, the town served as the U.S. capital in 1784 and 1799. Trenton became the state capital in 1790. The first state house opened in 1792. Many changes were made in the mid-1800s, but a fire in 1885 destroyed much of the capitol. Today's rebuilt capitol proudly honors its long history.

NEW MEXICO

Capital: Santa Fe

History:

The Spanish founded Santa Fe in 1607, thirteen years before the Pilgrims landed at Plymouth Rock. The city's first building, the Palace of the Governors, opened in 1610. This structure ranks as the nation's oldest public building in continuous use. It served as the capitol of the New Mexico territory until after the 1860s. Today it houses a museum. The historic city of Santa Fe attracts many tourists every year.

New York

Capital: Albany

History:

In 1624, Dutch settlers built Fort Orange on the banks of the Hudson River. Later renamed Albany, the town became the permanent state capital in 1797. The first capitol was replaced by a large ornate structure in 1899. Detailed carvings and the "Million Dollar Staircase" decorate the capitol. The New York State Museum, a theater and other buildings share the Empire State Plaza with the capitol. Visitors enjoy the view of the city from Corning Tower in the Plaza. The New York State Barge Canal System and the Hudson River meet at Albany, and Albany is also the eastern terminal of the Erie Canal.

North Carolina

Capital: Raleigh

History:

Raleigh became the North Carolina capital in 1788. The town was laid out four years later and work began on the first capitol. It burned in 1831 when workers who were fireproofing the building overturned a smelting pot. The present capitol opened in 1840. Stones on the outside walls weigh as much as ten tons each. No machines were used to place them—only muscle power from people and draft animals.

North Dakota

Capital: Bismarck

History:

The Dakota territory named Yankton its first capital in 1861. Bismarck's central location helped make it the permanent capital in 1883. The first capitol there opened in 1885 and burned in 1930. Money for new buildings was scarce during the Great Depression. Even so, the state built the "Skyscraper of the Prairies" in 1932. This capitol's striking 19-story tower is one of the state's prized landmarks today.

OHIO

Capital: Columbus

History:

In the 1800s, Columbus was a busy stagecoach stop. Its central location helped it become the state capital in 1812. Building the capitol took 22 years, from 1839 to 1861. Prisoners from the state jail laid the foundation and first floor. The exterior walls use limestone from the nearby Scioto River banks. Inside, a colorful dome spans 120 feet. A skylight brightens the center. Beneath the dome, nearly 5,000 pieces of hand-cut marble form the patterned floor. The 1996 Picnic with the Past brought some 20,000 people to the capitol to celebrate the building's restoration.

OKLAHOMA

Capital: Oklahoma City

History:

Oklahoma City was settled on April 22, 1889. That afternoon, thousands of people rushed to stake land claims there. The state's voters decided to move the capital from Guthrie to Oklahoma City in 1910. Lawmakers met in the Lee-Huckins Hotel until the first capitol was finished seven years later. Oklahoma City sits on an oil field. Many oil wells were dug around the city and even on the capitol grounds!

OREGON

Capital: Salem

History:

Missionaries founded Salem in 1840. The city became the state capital in 1864. Fires destroyed the first two capitols. The current four-story building opened in 1938. The gilded "Oregon Pioneer" statue at the capital's summit weighs 8.5 tons. It is hollow inside to keep it from weighing even more! A deck on the capitol's tower overlooks Salem's wide, tree-lined city streets and the pretty Willamette Valley.

PENNSYLVANIA
Capital: Harrisburg

History:

Settled by John Harris in 1718, Harrisburg grew as a ferry outpost on the Susquehanna River. Both Philadelphia and Lancaster served as capital cities before Harrisburg was named in 1812. The first capitol fell to fire in 1897. Today's capitol opened in 1906. Inspired by St. Peter's Basilica in Rome and the Paris Opera House, the capitol's planners created a grand building for the state's government. Its huge, column-lined dome looks out over the busy city. Gardens and parks on the riverbank invite afternoon strollers. Harrisburg's history, arts and natural beauty attract thousands of visitors every year.

RHODE ISLAND

Capital: Providence

History:

Roger Williams founded Providence in 1638 as a safe place for religious freedom. The harbor there helped the city grow. The city became Rhode Island's sole capital in 1900. A towering capitol with marble walls was finished in 1904. The "Independent Man" statue on its dome stands 235 feet above the terrace. This historic city in the smallest state remains one of New England's largest seaports.

SOUTH CAROLINA

Capital: Columbia

History:

In 1786, Columbia was founded with wide streets and quiet parks along the Congaree River. Its central location helped Columbia win the state capital honor. Mountain farmers felt that the first capital of Charleston favored "low country" plantation owners in the coastal plains. The farmers wanted a middle meeting place. Lawmakers chose Columbia in 1786 to ease the tension.

Workers laid the cornerstone for Columbia's capitol in 1851. Poor planning and weak materials slowed their progress. In 1865, work stopped as the Union army nearly destroyed the city. Columbia and its capitol were rebuilt after the Civil War. Today the state's largest city bustles with business, education and culture.

SOUTH DAKOTA

Capital: Pierre

History:

Pierre was the first capital of South Dakota. Many cities wanted the title, however. Pierre's central location helped it win a vote in 1904. A wooden capitol in Pierre hosted lawmakers until 1910. Today's capitol sits on a foundation of South Dakota boulder granite. Fancy marble walls and carved woodwork complete the inside. A solid-copper dome tops the building.

TENNESSEE

Capital: Nashville

History:

Settled in 1779, Fort Nashborough grew quickly along the banks of the Cumberland River. It took the name Nashville in 1784. The state made Nashville its permanent capital in 1843. The capitol opened in 1855. Today the tomb of President James K. Polk rests on the capitol grounds. Nearby, President Andrew Jackson's home attracts visitors. Tourists also flock to see the Grand Ole Opry and the many local Civil War battlefields.

TEXAS

Capital: Austin

History:

The Republic of Texas chose the village of Waterloo for its capital in 1839. The city was later renamed to honor colonizer Stephen F. Austin. Mexican and Indian raids forced the government to meet in Houston from 1842 to 1845. Work began on Austin's capitol in 1882. Set on a hillside above the Colorado River and spanning three acres, the state capitol building is the nation's largest. The "Goddess of Liberty" statue crowns the copper dome. The Capitol Extension, an underground addition to the main structure, opened in 1993. Connected by tunnels, it has hallways lined with skylights that provide a view of the dome.

UTAH

Capital: Salt Lake City

History:

Brigham Young led his Mormon followers to Salt Lake City in 1847. Pioneers stopped in the high desert town on their way to California. Mining and railroads also brought people there. Salt Lake City became the state capital in 1896. The capitol, the Mormon Temple, the Mormon Tabernacle and many other structures were built in the late 1800s and early 1900s. Today this historic city is a busy center for industry, education and culture.

VERMONT

Capital: Montpelier

History:

In 1787, settlers founded Montpelier in central Vermont. The city became the state capital in 1805. A simple, three-story capitol was built in 1808. A handsome capitol made of local granite blocks was finished in 1836. A fire reduced the building to rubble in 1857. Today's capitol opened in 1859 with palace-like decorations inside. The building's gilded dome overlooks historic Montpelier, the smallest capital in the U.S.

VIRGINIA

Capital: Richmond

History:

Virginia's history counts four capitols during the 1600s in Jamestown and two capitols in Williamsburg. Richmond was named the state capital in 1779. The British attacked the city in 1781, but the capitol looked so plain, the British didn't bother to burn it. Soon after the Revolutionary War, Thomas Jefferson designed a second and far more impressive capitol. This grand building, finished in 1785, still stands as the central part of today's modern capitol complex. As one of Virginia's largest cities, Richmond is an important center for commerce, education and the arts.

WASHINGTON

Capital: Olympia

History:

Settlers founded the town of Smithfield in 1846. The nearby Olympic Mountains inspired the name change to Olympia. In 1853, Olympia became the Washington territory's capital. It remained the capital after Washington gained statehood. Workers finished today's capitol in 1928. The 28-story building's grand dome overlooks Puget Sound. Thirty artisans created the beautiful carvings inside and a five-ton Tiffany chandelier graces the rotunda.

WEST VIRGINIA

Capital: Charleston

History:

West Virginia, the only state formed during the Civil War, chose Wheeling for its first capital. In 1870, the capital moved upriver to Charleston. Wheeling regained the title five years later. However, voters chose Charleston for the permanent capital in 1877. The capitol, opened in 1885, burned in 1921. Today's capitol opened in 1932. The state's largest city, Charleston now ranks as a U.S. leader in chemical and glass production.

WISCONSIN

Capital: Madison

History:

The Wisconsin territory named Madison as its capital in 1836, a year before the town was laid out. The first capitol opened in 1838. A larger building replaced it in 1863. A fire in 1904 made this second capitol useless. The towering dome of today's third capitol reigns over the Madison skyline. The grand white granite structure, built from 1906 to 1917, has a commanding view of two lakes—one to the east and one to the west.

WYOMING

Capital: Cheyenne

History:

As the Union Pacific Railroad pushed further into the frontier, squatters founded the camp of Cheyenne in 1867. The railroad's arrival fueled growth for the town. The Wyoming territory named Cheyenne as its capital in 1869. Cattle barons, cowboys and miners made the city a vital shipping and supply center for the West. Today, Cheyenne's majestic capitol offers tours that highlight the polished marble floors, detailed woodwork and colorful stained-glass windows.